Teeth Are Not for Biting

Teeth are strong and sharp.

Crunch!
Crunch!
Crunch!

Crunch! Crunch! Crunch!

Teeth can help you chew.

But teeth are not for biting.

Ouch! Biting hurts.

How many teeth
do you have?

You can count
them now.

Someday you
will have 20.

When new teeth grow,
your mouth may be sore.

When new teeth grow,
you may want to bite.

But teeth are not for biting.

Ouch! Biting hurts.

Let's do this instead:

Chew a chewy toy
Drink a cold drink
Take a little rest
Get a hug!

When you feel mad or sad,
you may want to bite.

But teeth are not for biting.
Ouch! Biting hurts.

Let's do this instead:

> Use your words
> Tell a grown-up
> Take a little break
> Get a hug!

Mmmmm...

that feels
better.

What if someone bites you? **Ouch!**

Do you bite back?
No. Biting hurts.

You can ask a
grown-up for help.

Teeth are not for biting.

Tips for Parents and Caregivers

Tips for teething

- Cuddle your child more often. Hugs and kisses help!

- Once they are weaned, give babies and toddlers frozen blueberries or peas to suck.

- Rub your child's gums with a clean finger.

- A cold, clean flannel, kept in the fridge is great for chomping on with sore gums.

- Talk to your health visitor or doctor to see if pain medications are a safe, effective option.

Tips for biting

- Toddlers and preschoolers are more prone to biting when they're teething, hungry, tired, upset, frustrated, angry, or bored. Watch for signs that a child may be uncomfortable or distressed, and try to help before biting even begins.

- Sometimes, toddlers bite to see how something tastes or feels in their mouth. This is a normal part of development. They may even bite to express affection. If this happens, you can gently but firmly say: "Ouch! Biting hurts. Please don't bite."

- Never bite your child back. This will hurt and frighten your child, and send the confusing message that biting is "okay" in some situations.

- Biting may occur when young children play or disagree. If it happens, first help the child who has been bitten. Offer hugs, comforting words, and any First Aid that may be needed. Next, you can focus your attention on the biter. Don't shout or scold. Calmly, briefly, and without anger, tell the child: "Teeth are not for biting. You hurt people when you bite." Give the child one or two minutes to calm down. Then redirect him or her to another activity.

- Young children may also bite to get attention. Use the above tips if biting occurs, but also consider ways to give positive attention at other times. You might point out, for example, when he or she is behaving well by using positive words.

First published in the UK in 2008 by Bloomsbury Publishing Plc
50 Bedford Square, London, WC1B 3DP
www.bloomsbury.com

ISBN 978-1-4081-1070-6

Original edition © 2006 by Free Spirit Publishing Inc., Minneapolis, U.S.A.,
http://www.freespirit.com under the title: Best Behaviour: Teeth are Not For Biting.
All rights reserved under International and Pan-American Copyright Conventions.

Printed in China by Leo Paper Products

This book is produced using paper that is made from wood grown in well-managed forests. It is natural, renewable and recyclable. The logging and manufacturing processes conform to the environmental regulations of the country of origin.

9 10